God's Word
Settled and Dependable

Dr Michael Andam

God's Word
Settled and Dependable

KDP

God's Word: Settled and Dependable
© 2019 Dr. Michael Andam

Published by KDP

Due to the nature of the Internet, any web addresses or links contained in this book may have changed since the publication and may not be valid.

Dedicated to
Dorcas, Elianne and Micaiah
God's word is indeed settled and always
dependable.

Content.

Preface---9
Chapter 1 A promise --------------------11
Chapter 2 The Word -------------------- 17
Chapter 3 Fulfilling Promise-----------29
Chapter 4 Human Promises-----------51
Chapter 5 Trust God-------------------- -57
Reference --------------------------------69

Preface

I have taken the steps to get to know Jesus Christ more and more each day in my walk with Him. I have come to realise that the more I get to know him the more I want like to know Him. The desire to know him and the hunger for that desire keep growing.

I came to the conclusion that because God is His word, this desire will continue to grow more and more as I read his word and understand what He is trying to relate to me through his word. The inspiration was to look at how God keeps His word. This could be seen as promises. There are times we could be facing so much difficult trials that we may tend to believe God can do all things but maybe for others and not for us.

In looking at God's promises to many starting from Adam, He has never changed. His word is still as potent as He is. He fulfills all His promises. The beauty of this is that He is able to make promises. The reason for making promises is that He always fulfills them. The Holy Spirit impressed on my heart to do a study on the book of Jeremiah. In calling Jeremiah into ministry, God showed him a vision, which is very significant to our understanding of God keeping His promises.

God showed Jeremiah an almond tree in this vision. In pursuing my understanding of scriptures, I ask questions and apply my acquired knowledge on biblical hermeneutics while depending on the Holy Spirit for answers. I asked why did God show him an almond tree and not an orange or olive tree? In my research, I came to the understanding of how important God watches over His word to perform it. That was the essence of the almond tree, watchfulness. God compared that to what He does with His word of promise to us. Let us study and have the understanding of the power of God's Word and how He fulfills all His promises.

1 A promise

What makes a promise?

What are the ingredients of a promise? What makes promise a promise? How do we distinguish a promise from a general statement? How do we differentiate a promise from anything else? What is a promise? Could a statement contain a promise?

A promise is first a commitment for someone to do or not to do something. In English expressions, it is a noun thus a declaration of assuring one will or will not do something. It is said that in the law of contract, a promise is said to be legally enforceable according to what is known as the Latin *maxim pacta sunt servanda*.

A promise could be seen as a statement of reassurance putting the credibility of the person on the line. Once that statement is given, one has become committed to fulfil it. It is the fundamental nature of that promise. Apart from the credibility of the person making that statement, words constitutes this statement and that is vital. Words once spoken cannot be reversed. Why is this very important?

Have you made a promise? Why did you make that promise? Note that making a promise does not necessarily start with the words 'I promise..." The nature of your statement will define this. For example, if you say " I will ensure this is fine by tomorrow and ensure this problem never occurs." It is the context at which we make certain statements that implies a commitment has been made. Such commitment constrains the recipient to hold the person accountable to fulfilling of such pronouncements.

Have you experienced a child's reaction to a promise? If you are not in a position to fulfill a promise to a child, simply don't make it. Promises from one person produce expectation from the recipient. Promises are usually made through words in whatever format presented. It could be by word of mouth, written or any other available format presented. Words are very powerful and we will get to know why this is so when we study why God made it so. Let us begin with promises from God.

Promises are made through words.
God makes His promises through His word. All of God's promises are interlinked with future generations to come. A promise could be made to an individual and that could be fulfilled several years later. It will be like unwrapping several layers on a present.

God's promises:
Adam and Eve: God created everything and on the sixth day created man in His own image. God instructed them on how to live this life He has given them. They were free to eat of every tree in the garden God housed them. There was one tree God asked them not to eat from. This was the tree of knowledge of good and evil. Their disobedience to this will bring about sin, as falling short of God's standard. The result of sin through disobedience was punishable by death.

The newly created man, male and female allowed the devil to entice and feed on their curiosity to live independent as gods and that caused them to go ahead and sin against God through disobedience. Once they sinned against God they realised that the words spoken to them by Satan through the serpent were absolutely lies. Jesus said that when Satan lies he does so from himself! He is full of lies and does not need to borrow.

God came to visit them. They heard the sound of the Lord walking in the garden and they hid themselves. God eventually got their attention and asked what they had done. God made plans for their redemption. He made the following statement:

Promise: "And I will put enmity between you and the woman, and between your seed and her Seed; He shall bruise your head, and you shall bruise His heel.""- Genesis 3:15.

God Almighty was referring to the coming of the Messiah to save Adam's race from the power of sin and death. The seed of the woman has been the Lord Jesus Christ and the serpent as Satan. Satan was to bruise the heel of the Messiah as history has recorded. However, the Messiah was to crush his head. This promise was made. Was it fulfilled right there? We will find out in the coming chapters when this was fulfilled.

God's promise to Noah: People begun to multiply on earth. The rate at which they continued sinning filled the earth with violence. God had to come down to investigate and see this level of sin for Himself. He decided to wipe out all the people He had created. One man called Noah found favour in God's eyes. God gave him some instructions on what to do to preserve species of animals from the coming flood. This flood was to wipe out all living creatures on earth.

　　After the flood, Noah and his family came out of the ark. Noah offered a thanksgiving offering to God for preserving his life. God was pleased with this offering and made him a promise:

Promise: "And the LORD smelled a soothing aroma. Then the LORD said in His heart, "I will never again curse the ground for man's sake, although the imagination of man's heart is evil from his youth; nor will I again destroy every living thing as I have done."-Genesis 8:21.

Following on from there God renewed His original blessings pronounced on Adam and Eve. "So God blessed Noah and his sons, and said to them: "Be fruitful and multiply, and fill the earth. And the fear of you and the dread of you shall be on every beast of the earth, on every bird of the air, on all that move on the earth, and on all the fish of the sea. They are given into your hand. Every moving thing that lives shall be food for you. I have given you all things, even as the green herbs."-Genesis 9:1-3.

God's promise to Abraham:
Promise: "Now the LORD had said to Abram: "Get out of your country, from your family and from your father's house, to a land that I will show you. I will make you a great nation; I will bless you and make your name great; and you shall be a blessing. I will bless those who bless you, and I will curse him who curses you; and in you all the families of the earth shall be blessed.""-Genesis 12:1-3.

Abraham, who was called Abram, received this great promise from God. It was given according to the spoken words of God.

God's promise to Isaac
"And I will make your descendants multiply as the stars of heaven; I will give to your descendants all these

lands; and in your seed all the nations of the earth shall be blessed;"-Genesis 26:4.

God clearly promised the son of Abraham as some point in time just as He did with his father.

God's promise to Jacob
"Behold, I am with you and will keep you wherever you go, and will bring you back to this land; for I will not leave you until I have done what I have spoken to you.""-Genesis 28:15.

God promised Jacob to bring him back to the land he found himself sleeping that night. He even used a stone as a pillow and yet had this vision with God making him this promise. God promised that He would be with him and keep him safe until this was fulfilled.

God's promise to Moses:
"Come now, therefore, and I will send you to Pharaoh that you may bring My people, the children of Israel, out of Egypt. "....So He said, "I will certainly be with you. And this shall be a sign to you that I have sent you: When you have brought the people out of Egypt, you shall serve God on this mountain.""-Exodus 3:10, 12.

Moses was given this huge task of leading a whole nation living in another country as slaves and to bring them out of bondage to freedom. He was to speak to Pharaoh, the most powerful leader at the time to ask him to free the children of Israel according to God's Word. Moses knew that was impossible as he was where God met him because he escaped from Egypt for the fear of his life. God promised to be with him. It was a surety, God said I will certainly be with you.

God's promise to Joshua

"Every place that the sole of your foot will tread upon I have given you, as I said to Moses.... No man shall be able to stand before you all the days of your life; as I was with Moses, so I will be with you. I will not leave you nor forsake you."-Joshua 1:3, 5.

After Moses died, Joshua was chosen to take over the reins. How was he going to fit into the shoes of such a great leader like Moses? The whole journey was focused on God and His children. God was not going to leave Joshua to be on his own to lead His people. He promised to be with him the same way he was with Moses. Absolutely great news to Joshua's hearing.

God's promise to Solomon

"At Gibeon the LORD appeared to Solomon in a dream by night; and God said, "Ask! What shall I give you?".... Therefore give to Your servant an understanding heart to judge Your people, that I may discern between good and evil. For who is able to judge this great people of Yours?""-I Kings 3:5, 9.

When Solomon took over from his father David, he loved the Lord and walked in the statutes according to a David. God appeared to him after he made a sacrifice unto Him. He gave him what we can describe as a 'blank cheque.' Solomon explains that he was grateful for God to put him on the throne and thus requested for wisdom to rule His people. What was God's response?

"The speech pleased the Lord, that Solomon had asked this thing. Then God said to him: "Because you have asked this thing, and have not asked long life for yourself, nor have asked riches for yourself, nor have asked the life of your enemies, but have asked for yourself understanding to discern justice, behold, I have done according to your words; see, I have given you a wise and understanding heart, so that there has not been anyone like you before you, nor shall any like you arise after you. And I have also given you what you have not asked: both riches and honour, so that there shall not be anyone like you among the kings all your days."-I Kings 3:10-13.

God's promise to us
Salvation. After Adam and Eve sinned against God by believing to become gods as suggested by the devil, God promised reconciliation. This was the promise of the Messiah to come and pay for the sins of humanity by crushing the head of Satan. "And I will put enmity between you and the woman, and between your seed and her Seed; He shall bruise your head, And you shall bruise His heel.""-Genesis 3:15.

Promise of the Holy Spirit.
Before Jesus ascended to heaven, He asked His followers to wait for the Father's promise of the Holy Spirit. "And being assembled together with them, He commanded them not to depart from Jerusalem, but to wait for the Promise of the Father, "which," He said, "you have heard from Me; for John truly baptised with water, but you shall be baptised with the Holy Spirit not many days from now.""-Acts 1:4-5.

Chapter

2 The Word

God's Word is settled in heaven

"Forever, O LORD, Your word is settled in heaven."-Psalms 119:89. The writer of this psalm concluded that the word of God is settled. What does it mean to be settled? The Meriam Webster dictionary explains this as 'to be fixed, established or concluded.' God has spoken and it is final. Nothing can be added or taken away from it.

Jesus is described as the Word in John's gospel. "In the beginning was the Word, and the Word was with God, and the Word was God. He was in the beginning with God. All things were made through Him, and without Him nothing was made that was made."-John 1:1-3. This means Jesus, as God is equal to His word. Whatever He says come to pass as it is settled in heaven.

The gospel writers recorded Jesus confirming that His word will not pass away. He is His word and as eternal God He will never cease to exist. The gospel writer Matthew recorded his version as follows: "Heaven and earth will pass away, but My words will by no means pass away."-Matthew 24:35. The gospel writer Mark also weighed in: "Heaven and earth will pass away, but My words will by no means pass away."-Mark 13:31.

The writer Luke, a physician would not be left out. He recorded at least two of such statements. "And it is easier for heaven and earth to pass away than for one tittle of the law to fail."-Luke 16:17. "Heaven and earth will pass away, but My words will by no means pass away."-Luke 21:33.

The importance of Word

God's Word is settled and so every word spoken must be established. God talks us through His plan by His word to enable us to understand and accept through faith.

Promises of and from God become more serious as it involves words. Why is this so important? God is His word. You cannot separate God from His word. He is His word. The creation account in Genesis gives us a good picture of God as His word. The beginning of the Bible reads as follow: "In the beginning God created the heavens and the earth....
Then God said, "Let there be light"; and there was light."-Genesis 1:1, 3.

In the beginning God created the heaven and the earth with the power of His word. God does not joke with His words, which are promises to us. The writer of psalms confirmed that God's Word brought everything into existence. He even breathed out the stars! "By the word of the LORD the heavens were made, and all the host of them by the breath of His mouth."-Psalms 33:6.

God's Word in action

God called a young man to be a prophet to His nation, His Children Israel. On the day He revealed the call to him, God made some awesome pronouncements that revealed how important His word is to Him.

This was what God said to this prophet as written by Jeremiah himself: "Then the word of the LORD came to me, saying: "Before I formed you in the womb I knew you; Before you were born I sanctified you; I ordained you a prophet to the nations.""-Jeremiah 1:4-5.

You would notice that it was God's word that came to him. The words categorically showed the nature of God's relationship with His children and how they should conduct themselves. It is Obvious that the young prophet Jeremiah understood this statement. He was called to appear before great and powerful rulers of the land to deliver God's messages including warnings to them. That is in every way scary and for a young person maybe even more frightening! He expressed his fears to the Lord. Let's make that into a conversation between Jeremiah and God Almighty.

Jeremiah: "...Ah, Lord GOD! Behold, I cannot speak, for I am a youth.""-Jeremiah 1:6

God: ..."Do not say, 'I am a youth,' for you shall go to all to whom I send you, and whatever I command you, you shall speak. Do not be afraid of their faces, for I am with you to deliver you," says the LORD."-Jeremiah 1:7-8.

God knew all about the young Jeremiah as we read. He knew him before conception and birth! Jeremiah's expression of inadequacy and fear did not take God by surprise. As a good Father, He went ahead to address all these fears one by one in a unique way.

God started to build the foundation of strength and stability for Jeremiah ministry. He said I will be with you. If the Creator of everything says that to you what other assurance do you need? We will get to understand these principles of God's word as we continue with our study. The fundamental principle to root out any fear and doubt is the fact that God is with us. That is the most powerful and valuable asset to have not forgetting the ultimate reassurance that brings.

First of all He dealt with the supernatural aspects. "Then the LORD put forth His hand and touched my mouth, and the LORD said to me: "Behold, I have put My words in your mouth."-Jeremiah 1:9. God was still touching on the subject of His word. It is vital to understand that the main focus in this dialogue with Jeremiah was about the word of God and it's delivery.

Moreover, this was also meant to reassure him that whatever God says to him was to be delivered without fearing the faces of the recipients. The good news is that God knows those He sends us to. Although we always feel inadequate, His presence makes the difference.

After this level of reassurance, God completes showing the task involved in Jeremiah's calling to be His prophet. "See, I have this day set you over the nations and over the kingdoms, to root out and to pull down, to destroy and to throw down, to build and to plant.""-Jeremiah 1:10. It was a pretty heavy task to bring about a total revolution. To destroy and throw down in order to rebuild is not an easy task.

Although God was not negotiating with Jeremiah, He was still interested in his acceptance of this calling. Why is this so? Couldn't anyone else perform this task? Of course God can use anyone. However, there is always the same response from all those He called till date? God calls us to do great things that are beyond our human abilities. The principle is that He partners with us to make this happen. We hear it and initially back down and run away from it!

Moreover, God respect the free will He gave us. He presents our purpose in life to us in ways that we are able to finally accept with His guidance and assurance as we studied earlier. At the end God wants a His purpose to be fulfilled to His glory.

Almond Tree-Watching over His Word to perform it
God went on to explain His stand with regards to His word. He showed Jeremiah a vision. Afterwards He asked Jeremiah to share what he saw in this vision.

"Moreover the word of the LORD came to me, saying, "Jeremiah, what do you see?" And I said, "I see a branch of an almond tree." Then the LORD said to me, "You have seen well, for I am ready to perform My word.""- Jeremiah 1:11-12

In this vision Jeremiah said he saw a branch of an almond tree. The Lord commented and said he had seen well and He was ready to perform His word. Other translations render it as watching over His word to fulfil it.

Why did God show him an almond tree and not any of the others like an apple tree? The Hebrew word for almond *'shakied'* that comes from the root which is to 'watch' that is *'shakad'.* It is known that the almond tree is among the first trees to "awaken" from its winter sleep. The vision given to Jeremiah with regards to the almond tree was to explain God's watchfulness and faithfulness with regards to His word. God is awake to watch over His word and perform it speedily. He is watching over His word to perform it.

We read that His word is established in heaven. He is not a man to go against His word. He cannot go against Himself as that will not make Him God. ""God is not a man, that He should lie, Nor a son of man, that He should repent. Has He said, and will He not do? Or has He spoken, and will He not make it good?"-Numbers 23:19. What an assurance from the King and Father!

Background of revelation

The background of why this revelation came out is very important. This happened when God's Word and strong hand delivered the children of Israel from Egypt. As the children of Israel were on their way to the Promised Land, they came near some enemy territories.

When they came near Moab, the people were scared stiff. They heard what Israel was doing to nations, as they possessed their possessions. "Then the children of Israel moved, and camped in the plains of Moab on the side of the Jordan across from Jericho."-Numbers 22:1

The king of Moab, Balak, obviously saw the people of Israel camping close by. "Now Balak the son of Zippor saw all that Israel had done to the Amorites. And Moab was exceedingly afraid of the people because they were many, and Moab was sick with dread because of the children of Israel. So Moab said to the elders of Midian, "Now this company will lick up everything around us, as an ox licks up the grass of the field." And Balak the son of Zippor was king of the Moabites at that time."-Numbers 22:2-4.

Did you see the description of how he perceived Israel would do to them? They will lick them up like an ox lick up grass from the field. This will not make any king comfortable. He devised a cunning plan.

"Then he sent messengers to Balaam the son of Beor at Pethor, which is near the River in the land of the sons of his people, to call him, saying: "Look, a people has come from Egypt. See, they cover the face of the earth, and are settling next to me! Therefore please come at once, curse this people for me, for they are too mighty for me. Perhaps I shall be able to defeat them and drive them out of the land, for I know that he whom you bless is blessed, and he whom you curse is cursed.""-Numbers 22:5-6.

Balaam was a prophet outside Israel. The messengers of king Balak brought the message from their king. He asked them to stay until he hears what God says. God came to Balaam and asked him some questions: "Then God came to Balaam and said, "Who are these men with you?" So Balaam said to God, "Balak the son of Zippor, king of Moab, has sent to me, saying, 'Look, a people has come out of Egypt, and they cover the face of the earth. Come now, curse them for me; perhaps I shall be able to overpower them and drive them out.' ""-Numbers 22:9-11.

God warned him not to go with them. The reason was that God has blessed Israel and they cannot be cursed. They were God's treasured children. No one can reverse God's Word. God blessed them and no one can turn back God's Word. "And God said to Balaam, "You shall not go with them; you shall not curse the people, for they are blessed.""-Numbers 22:12.

On another occasion Balaam was on his way when an angel of the Lord was sent to stop him. God found his ways to be perverse against the Lord. His donkey saw the angel and tried to avoid him. Three times Balaam struck the donkey. The angel opened the mouth of the donkey to speak. Had the donkey not stopped the angel would have killed Balaam.

He was led to speak only what God asked him to speak. Balak persuaded him to curse Israel persuaded on three occasions. Balaam could not curse Israel hence making that statement that God is not a man to lie. He blessed Israel and no one could reverse it.

""God is not a man, that He should lie, nor a son of man, that He should repent. Has He said, and will He not do? Or has He spoken, and will He not make it good? Behold, I have received a command to bless; He has blessed, and I cannot reverse it. "He has not observed iniquity in Jacob, nor has He seen wickedness in Israel. The LORD his God is with him, and the shout of a King is among them. God brings them out of Egypt; He has strength like a wild ox. "For there is no sorcery against Jacob, nor any divination against Israel. It now must be said of Jacob And of Israel, 'Oh, what God has done!'"- Numbers 23:19-23.

On the third occasion Balak was angry with Balaam. "Then Balak's anger was aroused against Balaam, and he struck his hands together; and Balak said to Balaam, "I called you to curse my enemies, and look, you have bountifully blessed them these three times!"-Numbers 24:10.

God's Word is final
The reason why God will unveil His calling over our life step by step and the reassurance of His presence is because His word is irreversible. Whatever He says in His plans must be accomplished exactly as He intends.
        The prophet Isaiah prophesied and showed us the perfect picture of how God's Word works.

""For as the rain comes down, and the snow from heaven, And do not return there, But water the earth, And make it bring forth and bud, That it may give seed to the sower And bread to the eater, So shall My word be that goes forth from My mouth; It shall not return to

Me void, But it shall accomplish what I please, And it shall prosper in the thing for which I sent it."-Isaiah 55:10-11.

In summary this is what happens when God send His word to accomplish anything.
- ♦ God sends His word regarding anything He wishes to accomplish.
- ♦ The word goes forth and shall not go back to God void. Nothing can destroy that sent word.
- ♦ The word accomplishes what God pleases.
- ♦ The end result of what God intended prospers because God intended it to be so.

God was using this straightforward analogy with the rain to reveal His nature with regards to His word to us. He showed us a phenomenon we are all familiar with. We don't see the rain being picked up, all of it and returning to the clouds and refusing to water the earth to bring forth growth of plants. Once God speak a word, it must accomplish whatever He intended or purposed. Is this not good news to us? Whatever promises we have in His word concerning us will be accomplished.

Once the assignment is given to you, it is now your purpose and thus responsibility to fulfill it. How? We are to work with God to help us fulfil His plan and purpose which He has given us. It is not to be accomplished by our strength!!

We should remember that although heaven and earth will pass away, His word will remain. "For all the promises of God in Him are yes, and in Him Amen, to the glory of God through us."-II Corinthians 1:20. His word is solidly established in heaven and they are in Him yes and Amen.

Chapter 3
Fulfilling promises

Faithfulness of God

We will explore to see if the promises we read in chapter one have been fulfilled or yet to be fulfilled. Before we continue one thing is certain, God is faithful and always do whatever He says He will do. The first promise was to Adam and Eve with regards to the coming of the Messiah to reconcile us back to God.

Promise of a Messiah: Adam lived to be 939 years. This promise was not fulfilled during Adam's lifetime. He was almost a thousand years! Can you imagine waiting for God's promise for such a long time? You might as well give up and say it may never happen. However, God fulfilled His promise thousands of years after according to His divine plan and time.

At some point in time, the prophet Isaiah prophesied about some details of the coming Messiah. "Therefore the Lord Himself will give you a sign: Behold, the virgin shall conceive and bear a Son, and shall call His name Immanuel."-Isaiah 7:14. It still took some more hundreds of years before the promise was fulfilled. This did not happen during this prophet's lifetime. That hearing it over and over again might have thought this was never going to happen.

"But when the fullness of the time had come, God sent forth His Son, born of a woman, born under the law, to redeem those who were under the law, that we might receive the adoption as sons."-Galatians 4:4-

5. Baby Jesus was born after the angelic visit to Mary and Joseph, His earthly chosen parents.

God fulfilled one part of the promise for the Messiah to be the seed of a woman. The prophet Isaiah's prophesy was fulfilled. "So all this was done that it might be fulfilled which was spoken by the Lord through the prophet, saying: "Behold, the virgin shall be with child, and bear a Son, and they shall call His name Immanuel," which is translated, "God with us.""-Matthew 1:22-23.

The Bible recorded that when the fullness of time had come, God acted on His promise. It is all to do with God's plan and most importantly His timing.

Process of fulfilling promise

When Jesus started His ministry, He spoke about His mission openly right from the beginning. He was focused to accomplish what was planned right from the beginning. The gospel of Mark recorded at least three occasions whereby Jesus informed His disciples of His impending death and resurrection.

He did that through His teachings. "And He began to teach them that the Son of Man must suffer many things, and be rejected by the elders and chief priests and scribes, and be killed, and after three days rise again. He spoke this word openly. Then Peter took Him aside and began to rebuke Him."-Mark 8:31-32.

On another occasion He taught them again the importance of both the death and the resurrection. However, the disciples did not understand. "For He taught His disciples and said to them, "The Son of Man is being betrayed into the hands of men, and they will kill Him. And after He is killed, He will rise the third day." But they did not understand this saying, and were afraid to ask Him."-Mark 9:31-32.

On another occasion He gave them details of the cruelty He was about to suffer at the hands of sinners. The good news of His resurrection is still the focal point. "Now they were on the road, going up to Jerusalem, and Jesus was going before them; and they were amazed. And as they followed they were afraid. Then He took the twelve aside again and began to tell them the things that would happen to Him: "Behold, we are going up to Jerusalem, and the Son of Man will be betrayed to the chief priests and to the scribes; and they will condemn Him to death and deliver Him to the Gentiles; and they will mock Him, and scourge Him, and spit on Him, and kill Him. And the third day He will rise again.""-Mark 10:32-34

It is finished
All that Jesus told His disciples happened exactly as He told them. Jesus was crucified to fulfil all the promises and prophecies that came with it. "And they brought Him to the place Golgotha, which is translated, Place of a Skull. Then they gave Him wine mingled with myrrh to drink, but He did not take it. And when they crucified Him, they divided His garments, casting lots for them to determine what every man should take."-Mark 15:22-24.

On the cross, Jesus shouted with a voice of triumph and said all that He came to accomplish was finished. The price of Adam's sin was atoned by the shedding of Jesus Christ's blood. "And when Jesus had cried out with a loud voice, He said, "Father, 'into Your hands I commit My spirit.' " Having said this, He breathed His last."-Luke 23:46. "So when Jesus had received the sour wine, He said, "It is finished!" and bowing His head, He gave up His spirit."-John 19:30.

Promise fulfilled

The promise in Genesis 3:15 said the devil will strike the heel of the Messiah. That is exactly what we read until Jesus said it was finished.

Jesus was to crush the head of Satan during this encounter, which He did. Jesus paid the price of sin in full once and for all to redeem us. That brought the total defeat of the kingdom of darkness. Jesus totally destroyed them and made a public display of their defeat.

This is how describes this: "having wiped out the handwriting of requirements that was against us, which was contrary to us. And He has taken it out of the way, having nailed it to the cross. Having disarmed principalities and powers, He made a public spectacle of them, triumphing over them in it."-Colossians 2:14-15.

To crown it all, Jesus Christ resurrected triumphantly from the dead! This whole process from the time this promise was made till fulfillment took some thousands of years. As we know Adam lived to be almost a thousand years to start with. Scholars have calculated the years from Adam's creation and the birth of Christ to be around 4000 years using various historical data available.

The point here is that God will fulfil His promise according to His timing and purpose. It does not matter if the individuals promised are directly involved with the final execution or not. God created us to live in generations. One generation passes on to the next hence a promise could be fulfilled in a future generation.

Noah's promise

"And the LORD smelled a soothing aroma. Then the LORD said in His heart, "I will never again curse the ground for man's sake, although the imagination of man's heart is evil from his youth; nor will I again destroy every living thing as I have done. "While the earth remains, seedtime and harvest, Cold and heat, winter and summer, and day and night shall not cease.""-Genesis 8:21-22.

Since Noah's flood, God has kept His promises. There has not been rain over the whole earth just like what happened during Noah's time. We still have seedtime and harvest time. We still have all the seasons intact. We still experience day and night.

God's Word to Abraham

The third example in our study is the promise made to Abram. God changed his name to reflect the meaning that goes with the change of his destiny. God appeared to Abram and asked him to leave his hometown and his wider family network to a place He will show him. The following was what God said to him:

"Now the LORD had said to Abram: "Get out of your country, from your family and from your father's house, to a land that I will show you. I will make you a great nation; I will bless you and make your name great; and you shall be a blessing. I will bless those who bless you, and I will curse him who curses you; and in you all the families of the earth shall be blessed.""-Genesis 12:1-3.

God who had all the power was asking this man to first get out of his country to a land He will show him. He was going to make him a great nation. He was going to bless and make his name great and cause him to be a blessing. God was going to act on his behalf and either bless or curse anyone who does either to him. God was going to bless all the families of the earth in him. What an awesome words of promises from the creator of all things to a mortal man!

Abram must have known in his spirit that this was definitely the God of all creation speaking these powerful words of promises to him. It would be that encounter when you know for sure this must be God even when you do not know or serve Him. It doesn't matter, as He is still the Creator of all flesh whether we choose to accept Him or profess to be atheist. It doesn't change Him and how He operates.

Did Abram obey? Yes He did and moved according to God's direction. "So Abram departed as the LORD had spoken to him, and Lot went with him. And Abram was seventy-five years old when he departed from Haran. Then Abram took Sarai his wife and Lot his brother's son, and all their possessions that they had gathered, and the people whom they had acquired in Haran, and they departed to go to the land of Canaan. So they came to the land of Canaan. Abram passed through the land to the place of Shechem, as far as the terebinth tree of Moreh. And the Canaanites were then in the land."-Genesis 12:4-6.

Abram brought Lot with him. The blessing God promised Abram was so evident as there was so much increase in his possessions together with Lot's that the land they were dwelling was not big enough. "Now the land was not able to support them, that they might dwell together, for their possessions were so great that they could not dwell together."
-Genesis 13:6.

God took some time to unravel the promises step by step. He was also testing Abraham's faith along the way as He revealed His plans and purposes to him. Abram and his wife were very old with Sarai (changed to Sarah) passing the age of having children. God started unveiling his promises to them. "After these things the word of the LORD came to Abram in a vision, saying, "Do not be afraid, Abram. I am your shield, your exceedingly great reward." But Abram said, "Lord GOD, what will You give me, seeing I go childless, and the heir of my house is Eliezer of Damascus?""-Genesis 15:1-2.

Abram tried to reason and help God by using his human level of reasoning. God rejected his help in this perceived impossible situation. God is the Creator and nothing was impossible for Him. "And behold, the word of the LORD came to him, saying, "This one shall not be your heir, but one who will come from your own body shall be your heir." Then He brought him outside and said, "Look now toward heaven, and count the stars if you are able to number them." And He said to him, "So shall your descendants be." And he believed in the LORD, and He accounted it to him for righteousness."-Genesis 15:4-6.

Abraham did something that we should all practice especially at the face of extreme trials that seems impossible. He trusted and believed in the word of God. God accounted this to him as righteousness. What an honour. God went further to prove to him that He honours his promises. As there is no one higher than God, He promises by Himself and that is putting His reputation as God on the line.

Covenant God put His reputation on the line.
God made a covenant with Abraham putting His reputation on the line. "Then He said to him, "I am the LORD, who brought you out of Ur of the Chaldeans, to give you this land to inherit it."...So He said to him, "Bring Me a three-year-old heifer, a three-year-old female goat, a three-year-old ram, a turtledove, and a young pigeon." Then he brought all these to Him and cut them in two, down the middle, and placed each

piece opposite the other; but he did not cut the birds in two. -"Genesis 15:7, 9-10.

"And it came to pass, when the sun went down and it was dark, that behold, there appeared a smoking oven and a burning torch that passed between those pieces. On the same day the LORD made a covenant with Abram, saying: "To your descendants I have given this land, from the river of Egypt to the great river, the River Euphrates— the Kenites, the Kenezzites, the Kadmonites, the Hittites, the Perizzites, the Rephaim, the Amorites, the Canaanites, the Girgashites, and the Jebusites.""-Genesis 15:17-21. This was how people made binding covenant at the time. They cut animals in half and pass fire through it.

Abraham: Fulfilling of promise
Final details of step one toward the promise descendants. God worked a miracle for a 90-year-old woman and 100 years old to have a special child of covenant. "And He said, "I will certainly return to you according to the time of life, and behold, Sarah your wife shall have a son." (Sarah was listening in the tent door, which was behind him.) Now Abraham and Sarah were old, well advanced in age; and Sarah had passed the age of childbearing. Therefore Sarah laughed within herself, saying, "After I have grown old, shall I have pleasure, my lord being old also?"-Genesis 18:10-12

"And the LORD visited Sarah as He had said, and the LORD did for Sarah as He had spoken. For Sarah conceived and bore Abraham a son in his old age, at the set time of which God had spoken to him. And Abraham called the name of his son who was born to him—whom Sarah bore to him— Isaac. Now Abraham was one hundred years old when his son Isaac was born to him. And Sarah said, "God has made me laugh, and all who hear will laugh with me." She also said,

"Who would have said to Abraham that Sarah would nurse children? For I have borne him a son in his old age.""-Genesis 21:1-3, 5-7

At the time of Abraham's death the nation of Israel had not been formed. However, God fulfilled every promise to Abraham even after his death. God was responsible for His word and watched over it to fulfil it. God fulfilled the raising of a nations part of the promises through his son Isaac, Ishmael and mainly Jacob. God changed Jacob's name to Israel. The meaning was changed from a supplanter to the prince of God.

Abraham's seed to be slaves for 400 years.
In between the making of the covenant we just read, God informed Abraham that the promised seed would be slaves in a foreign land for **four hundred years.** "Now when the sun was going down, a deep sleep fell upon Abram; and behold, horror and great darkness fell upon him. Then He said to Abram: "Know certainly that your descendants will be strangers in a land that is not theirs, and will serve them, and they will afflict them four hundred years. And also the nation whom they serve I will judge; afterward they shall come out with great possessions."-Genesis 15:12-14

There was a second part to this revelation. Although his descendants would become slaves for 400 years God would deliver them afterwards. This was what God said to Abraham: "But in the fourth generation they shall return here, for the iniquity of the Amorites is not yet complete.""-Genesis 15:16. God is patient and slow to anger. He was going to wait until the iniquity of the Amorites were complete to drive them out of the occupied Promised Land.

God also promised that Abraham would live many years. "Now as for you, you shall go to your fathers in peace; you shall be buried at a good old age. But in the fourth generation they shall return here, for the iniquity of the Amorites is not yet complete.""- Genesis 15:15-16. God promised that after four hundred years his descendants would return to the land he was dwelling at present.

Nations through Isaac

"Now Isaac pleaded with the LORD for his wife, because she was barren; and the LORD granted his plea, and Rebekah his wife conceived. But the children struggled together within her; and she said, "If all is well, why am I like this?" So she went to inquire of the LORD. And the LORD said to her: "Two nations are in your womb, two peoples shall be separated from your body; one people shall be stronger than the other, and the older shall serve the younger.""-Genesis 25:21-23.

From Isaac, the covenant son of Abraham, God begun unfolding the promises He made to Abraham. God described the twins born to Isaac as two nations. One of the two sons named Jacob became Israel and fulfilled God's promise of Abraham's seed becoming slaves in a nation for four hundred years.

Jacob gave birth to 12 sons. One was called Joseph. His brothers hatred him for two dreams he shared with them. The dreams symbolised he ruling over them. The father also made the matter worse by showing favouritism. He made Joseph a coat of many colours. One day the dad sent him to check on his brothers who were looking after the sheep. They saw him afar off and some plotted to kill him and see what becomes of those dreams of leadership. Finally some of the brothers saw it best to make profit out of him by selling him to some merchants instead of killing him.

Joseph was brought to Egypt and sold to one of the King's guard. Joseph went through a series of harsh trials and temptations but stood to continue to trust in his God. The great news was that God was with him throughout this journey and everything he did prospered. He was promoted even when he was put in prison on false allegations. God allowed two of pharaoh's top officials to be put in the prison where Joseph was. He was assigned by the warden to serve these high-ranking officials. They both had dreams one day and looked sad the next morning. By the power of God Joseph interpreted their dreams. It happened exactly as God through Joseph interpreted. One was killed and the other called back to service.

He forgot all about Joseph until after two years when the king dreamt and needed interpreting. The official remembered Joseph and he was brought out to meet the king. After God's power to interpret the dreams, he was promoted as next in command to Pharaoh! Pharaoh asked Joseph to bring his extended family to Egypt. A portion of land was allocated to them when the dad and the brothers came to live there.

Promise of divine visitation

The family of Jacob grew into the nation God promised Abraham and now Jacob. This is what God said when Pharaoh invited them to leave Canaan to Egypt. "Then God spoke to Israel in the visions of the night, and said, "Jacob, Jacob!" And he said, "Here I am." So He said, "I am God, the God of your father; do not fear to go down to Egypt, for I will make of you a great nation there. I will go down with you to Egypt, and I will also surely bring you up again; and Joseph will put his hand on your eyes.""-Genesis 46:2-4.

They grew in number as the generations were born. Before Joseph died, he assured them of God visiting and taking them to the Promised Land. "And Joseph said to his brethren, "I am dying; but God will surely visit you, and bring you out of this land to the land of which He swore to Abraham, to Isaac, and to Jacob.""-Genesis 50:24. He asked them to carry his bones with them when the time comes.

The children of Israel were fruitful and continued to multiply greatly in the land. "But the children of Israel were fruitful and increased abundantly, multiplied and grew exceedingly mighty; and the land was filled with them."-Exodus 1:7. A new king arose who did not know Joseph. He became afraid of the children of Israel with regards to their number and strength. "Now there arose a new king over Egypt, who did not know Joseph. And he said to his people, "Look, the people of the children of Israel are more and mightier than we; come, let us deal shrewdly with them, lest they multiply, and it happen, in the event of war, that they also join our enemies and fight against us, and so go up out of the land.""-Exodus 1:8-10.

God and Moses.
Moses was born at the time the people of Israel were under bondage in ancient Egypt as we just read. The king of Egypt decided to kill all Hebrew baby boys, as he was afraid of how strong they were growing. He was scared they would join an enemy to attack Egypt. He enslaved the people of Israel living in Egypt.

The mother of Moses devised a way to save the baby from being killed. She put him in a waterproof basket and placed it in the side of the Nile River where the king's daughter visits. It did happen and the princess took the baby to the palace. Before then, Moses' sister waited until the princess found him and she came to ask if she can get someone to nurse the baby for the princess. The plan worked and the mum took care of him till old enough to go to the palace.

Moses grew up as a prince of Egypt. He got to know his roots as one of the people enslaved. In his quest to save his people he killed an Egyptian. The case became known and Pharaoh was after Moses to kill him. Moses went into exile for forty years. He was looking after the sheep of a man called Jethro, a priest, who became his father in law.

He was going about his normal routine taking the sheep for pasture when he had a supernatural encounter with God. Let's see if God used the word of promise. "Now Moses was tending the flock of Jethro his father-in-law, the priest of Midian. And he led the flock to the back of the desert, and came to Horeb, the mountain of God. And the Angel of the LORD appeared to him in a flame of fire from the midst of a bush. So he looked, and behold, the bush was burning with fire, but the bush was not consumed. Then Moses said, "I will now turn aside and see this great sight, why the bush does not burn." So when the LORD saw that he turned aside to look, God called to him from the midst of the bush and said, "Moses, Moses!" And he said, "Here I am.""-Exodus 3:1-4.

Dialogue

Once again God was unveiling His plan and at the same time fulfilling His promises made to Abraham. It was a kind of fulfilling a series of promises from old right up to current ones made. The Lord appears to Moses and send him to pharaoh with specific requests from God.

"And the LORD said: "I have surely seen the oppression of My people who are in Egypt, and have heard their cry because of their taskmasters, for I know their sorrows.... Now therefore, behold, the cry of the children of Israel has come to Me, and I have also seen the oppression with which the Egyptians oppress them."-Exodus 3:7, 9.

It would have sounded really good to Moses. Help was finally at hand. Moses may have been absolutely elated! God then said something else which hit all the attention of Moses. "Come now, therefore, and I will send you to Pharaoh that you may bring My people, the children of Israel, out of Egypt.""-Exodus 3:10.

Moses response is one that echoes through history anytime God chooses an ordinary person to partner with Him to do extraordinary and supernatural tasks impossible for the human kind. "But Moses said to God, "Who am I that I should go to Pharaoh, and that I should bring the children of Israel out of Egypt?""-Exodus 3:11.

God knows His timings and when to implement His plans as He watches over His word to fulfil them. These eternal words come as promises and miracles to people He spoke to. God reassured Moses of the ultimate security one could ever get. This is to have the Creator of everything visible and invisible to be with you. "So He said, "I will certainly be with you. And this shall be a sign to you that I have sent you: When you have brought the people out of Egypt, you shall serve God on this mountain.""-Exodus 3:12.

Possessions: God said to Abraham that his descendants would come out of slavery with great possessions. "And the LORD said to Moses, "I will bring one more plague on Pharaoh and on Egypt. Afterward he will let you go from here. When he lets you go, he will surely drive you out of here altogether. Speak now in the hearing of the people, and let every man ask from his neighbour and every woman from her neighbour, articles of silver and articles of gold." And the LORD gave the people favour in the sight of the Egyptians. Moreover the man Moses was very great in the land of Egypt, in the sight of Pharaoh's servants and in the sight of the people."-Exodus 11:1-3.

In order to come out of the land that oppressed them with greet possessions, God had to place them there. The reason He told Abraham that would happen.

After the tenth plague in Egypt at the time, the children of Israel were literally driven out of the land. Everything seemed to be going well until the faced the Red Sea. Pharaoh had changed his mind and set the best soldiers after them.

Fulfilling of 400year promise

The people saw the enemy and naturally were very much afraid. The protective hand of God did not leave them. The angel who was leading them now went behind them. There was also a pillar of cloud that went in front of them. The pillar also went behind them. "...So it came between the camp of the Egyptians and the camp of Israel. Thus it was a cloud and darkness to the one, and it gave light by night to the other, so that the one did not come near the other all that night."-Exodus 14:19-20.

God was not about to leave them on the final hour to see His glory and greatness manifested.

"And Moses said to the people, "Do not be afraid. Stand still, and see the salvation of the LORD, which He will accomplish for you today. For the Egyptians whom you see today, you shall see again no more forever.... And the LORD said to Moses, "Why do you cry to Me? Tell the children of Israel to go forward. But lift up your rod, and stretch out your hand over the sea and divide it. And the children of Israel shall go on dry ground through the midst of the sea."-Exodus 14:13, 15-16.

Moses obeyed and the promise to Abraham with regards to his descendants coming out of bondage with great possessions after 400 years was fulfilled. The scripture total the years to be 430. Once again there are various explanations to fit it into the promise of God with various calculations to explain it.

God saved Israel from the armies of pharaoh when He opened up the Red Sea for them to walk through to safely. Moses stretched the rod over the parted sea as commanded by God and the waters came back and destroyed Pharaoh's army. "So the LORD saved Israel that day out of the hand of the Egyptians, and Israel saw the Egyptians dead on the seashore. Thus Israel saw the great work which the LORD had done in Egypt; so the people feared the LORD, and believed the LORD and His servant Moses."-Exodus 14:30-31.

Moses took them out of bondage. Was he going to fulfill the other part of Gods promise to Abraham, Isaac and Jacob? Did he bring them in? Did God fulfill His promise?

We are dealing with huge fulfillment of promises concerning a whole nation. There were so many people, steps and years involved. This means it does not necessarily involve the original person the promise was made to as we read earlier. In Abraham's case God was specific to point out that it involved those after him, his descendants.

Back to the Promised Land to Abraham Joshua.

After so many acts of disobedience to God, one generation had to die before their children were permitted to enter the Promised Land. This happened when Moses sent 12 spies to check the land out before they took over. Ten came with bad report that destroyed the morale and faith of the people. It was only Joshua and Caleb who encouraged the people to trust in God's word and go and possess the land immediately. They did not listen to them. God promised that only Joshua and Caleb from that generation will enter the Promised Land. Moses and that generation all died.

"After the death of Moses the servant of the LORD, it came to pass that the LORD spoke to Joshua the son of Nun, Moses' assistant, saying: "Moses My servant is dead. Now therefore, arise, go over this Jordan, you and all this people, to the land which I am giving to them—the children of Israel. Every place that the sole of your foot will tread upon I have given you, as I said to Moses. From the wilderness and this Lebanon as far as the great river, the River Euphrates, all the land of the Hittites, and to the Great Sea toward the going down of the sun, shall be your territory. No man shall be able to stand before you all the days of your life; as I was with Moses, so I will be with you. I will not leave you nor forsake you."-Joshua 1:1-5

God promised to be with Joshua the same way He was with Moses. God instructed him to go ahead to possess the land promised Abraham's descendants. "Now Joshua the son of Nun sent out two men from Acacia Grove to spy secretly, saying, "Go, view the land, especially Jericho." So they went, and came to the house of a harlot named Rahab, and lodged there."-Joshua 2:1.

It became evidential that the people of Israel were conquering nations upon nations as they drew closer to those occupying their land. "So it was, when all the kings of the Amorites who were on the west side of the Jordan, and all the kings of the Canaanites who were by the sea, heard that the LORD had dried up the waters of the Jordan from before the children of Israel until we had crossed over, that their heart melted; and there was no spirit in them any longer because of the children of Israel."-Joshua 5:1.

One by one, Joshua and Israel conquered nations occupying their God given Promised Land. Jericho, Ai and all the rest, they shared it among the tribes. They inherited what God promised Abraham, Isaac and Jacob.

The great leader Joshua also emphasised the fact that God fulfilled all His promises to Israel in his lifetime. ""Behold, this day I am going the way of all the earth. And you know in all your hearts and in all your souls that not one thing has failed of all the good things which the LORD your God spoke concerning you. All have come to pass for you; not one word of them has failed."-Joshua 23:14.

Solomon. Wisdom promise fulfilled.
Solomon was granted his request to have wisdom to rule and serve God's people. He presided over some cases such as the two women with the case of a dead child. Solomon exercised his given wisdom to judge this. "And all Israel heard of the judgment which the king had rendered; and they feared the king, for they saw that the wisdom of God was in him to administer justice."-I Kings 3:28.

"And God gave Solomon wisdom and exceedingly great understanding, and largeness of heart like the sand on the seashore."-I Kings 4:29. Notice the writing here, God gave him as a way to fulfill His promise to him. God fulfilled His promises by giving us more than we can ever imagine or ask.

"Thus Solomon's wisdom excelled the wisdom of all the men of the East and all the wisdom of Egypt. For he was wiser than all men—than Ethan the Ezrahite, and Heman, Chalcol, and Darda, the sons of Mahol; and his fame was in all the surrounding nations."-I Kings 4:30-31.

The impact of this divine given wisdom brought people from all over to come and hear King Solomon. "And men of all nations, from all the kings of the earth who had heard of his wisdom, came to hear the wisdom of Solomon."-I Kings 4:34.

Riches: Combination of wisdom and riches

"And these governors, each man in his month, provided food for King Solomon and for all who came to King Solomon's table. There was no lack in their supply. They also brought barley and straw to the proper place, for the horses and steeds, each man according to his charge."-I Kings 4:27-28. "The weight of gold that came to Solomon yearly was six hundred and sixty-six talents of gold, besides that from the traveling merchants, from the income of traders, from all the kings of Arabia, and from the governors of the country."-I Kings 10:14-15.

We cannot comment on all the riches God divinely gave to King Solomon as He promised. Remember God said He would give him riches because he only asked for wisdom to rule His people. The scripture above is one of many that tell of the extent of Solomon's riches in all areas of life. This was a combination of wisdom and riches. He used his wisdom to effect a potent administrative government. In that case the resources were managed well and not wasted.

The Queen of Sheba heard of the greatness of this king's wisdom and wealth. She planned to test his wisdom by asking some pretty difficult questions. She visited Solomon and he answered all her questions to her amazement. Now this was her reaction as recorded in the book of King's.

"And when the queen of Sheba had seen all the wisdom of Solomon, the house that he had built, the food on his table, the seating of his servants, the service of his waiters and their apparel, his cupbearers, and his entryway by which he went up to the house of the LORD, there was no more spirit in her. Then she said to the king: "It was a true report which I heard in my own land about your words and your wisdom. However I did not believe the words until I came and saw with my own eyes; and indeed the half was not told me. Your wisdom and prosperity exceed the fame of which I heard."-I Kings 10:4-7.

It was not only the great Queen of Sheba who came to hear of Solomon's wisdom. Everyone in the known world at the time did too. All those who came to hear him did not come empty handed. They came with presents to the king who was already divinely blessed with material wealth as well as wisdom. "Now all the earth sought the presence of Solomon to hear his wisdom, which God had put in his heart. Each man brought his present: articles of silver and gold, garments, armor, spices, horses, and mules, at a set rate year by year."-I Kings 10:24-25.

Promises to us
The promise to Adam and Eve that we read was a promise to us as well. In our time, this promise has been fulfilled. Jesus had done it all by paying the price of sin. We are **not created** to be little gods as Adam and Eve wanted to become when the devil deceived them.

We are to become children of God once again as Adam and Eve were. Let's look at one scripture that describes Adam as a child of God and **not gods**. In the gospel of Luke's record of genealogy of Jesus Christ, he placed Adam as the son of God. "...the son of Enosh, the son of Seth, the son of Adam, the son of God."-Luke 3:38.

Jesus came to die for our sins so whoever accepts His free gift of life becomes a child of the Almighty God. The promise to be reborn into the family of God is open to all who believe, accept and live accordingly. "But as many as received Him, to them He gave the right to become children of God, to those who believe in His name: who were born, not of blood, nor of the will of the flesh, nor of the will of man, but of God."-John 1:12-13.

Chapter 4

Human promises

No contest

I chose to take a look at how we sometimes make the biggest error in life by comparing situations or even characters with that of God Almighty. There are times we could be tempted to think God behaves exactly as our parents or people we look up to. There are times that we may all fail to honour things said that may look as a promise. Some of us made conscious effort to avoid this. Rather than making a promise we say we will see what we can do. Just to avoid the claws of a promise. It could even apply to executives in authority.

For instance, it has become a common knowledge that most politicians never answer pressing questions. Most embarrassingly many are seen as liars. Their words are not worth anything to many citizens. Even when they fail to do what they promised, going to the moon and back would appear easier than for many politicians to say 'sorry we couldn't get that right.' Many could mistaken God's leadership, as King of king's to equate to this level of unfaithfulness. From what we have studied so far, it is clear that God always honours His word. He continues to do so until the last day and throughout eternity.

We must never compare anyone to God. He is His word. Whatever He has said in His word is in Him yes and in Him, Amen. If He says He can save and heal you, that is what He will do. Now let us look as few examples of human promises and the outcome. We will see how these were not honoured as the outcome.

Satan and Adam/Eve

Satan, using the serpent's voice promised them that they will not surely die if they eat from the tree God commanded them not to do so. Satan said they will become gods if they eat from this tree. Adam and Eve believed in this promise from Satan and lost everything. They did not become gods. Their eyes open to the world of sin, shame and death.

Laban promises Jacob

Jacob, the son of Isaac and grandson of Abraham went to live with his mother's brother Laban. Laban asked Jacob to name his wages for working for him, which he did. "Then Laban said to Jacob, "Because you are my relative, should you therefore serve me for nothing? Tell me, what should your wages be? ""-Genesis 29:15.

Jacob made known what he wanted as his wages in line with the request from Laban, his uncle. "Now Jacob loved Rachel; so he said, "I will serve you seven years for Rachel your younger daughter.""-Genesis 29:18. Jacob served for seven years as though that was nothing because of his love for Rachel. I believe many who fell in love would understand this. Did Laban honour his promise after seven years?

They followed the marriage custom where you do not see the face of the bride in you room till the next morning. That is how it appeared from Jacobs's shock experienced in the morning. "So it came to pass in the morning, that behold, it was Leah. And he said to Laban, "What is this you have done to me? Was it not for Rachel that I served you? Why then have you deceived me?""-Genesis 29:25. How would you call this? Remember he served seven years of his life for Rachel!

What was the explanation or excuse from Laban? "And Laban said, "It must not be done so in our country, to give the younger before the firstborn. Fulfill her week, and we will give you this one also for the service which you will serve with me still another seven years.""-Genesis 29:26-27. So the question is why did he not inform him at the beginning of the seven-year service? He could have said this before deceiving him after seven years of service. Now Rachel was given to him as well. He has two wives! On top of this he had to work another seven years for that.

The deception went on for a while with Jacob using wisdom from God to obtain legitimate wealth. He made a statement that suggested Laban's continuous unfaithfulness when it came to honouring promises. "And you know that with all my might I have served your father. Yet your father has deceived me and changed my wages ten times, but God did not allow him to hurt me."-Genesis 31:6-7.

Peter, Jesus and the rest of disciples
After Jesus instituted the Lord's Supper, He warned them of what was coming. He was about to be betrayed into the hands of sinners as He had told them several times. The time was up. He said they will all scatter and desert Him. Let us put this scripture in a conversation format:

Jesus: "...All of you will be made to stumble because of Me this night, for it is written: 'I will strike the Shepherd, And the sheep of the flock will be scattered.' But after I have been raised, I will go before you to Galilee.""-Matthew 26:31-32. Peter was quick to respond to this as one of the three closest friends in the inner circles of Jesus.

Peter: "...Even if all are made to stumble because of You, I will never be made to stumble.""-Matthew 26:33. Notice his boldness making this declaration. He said he will not stumble even if all were made to do so because of whatever happens.

Jesus:"...Assuredly, I say to you that this night, before the rooster crows, you will deny Me three times.""-Matthew 26:34. Peter did not give up. He went further to say that even if it meant for him to die with Jesus he will not deny Him.

Peter and the rest: "Peter said to Him, "Even if I have to die with You, I will not deny You!" And so said all the disciples."-Matthew 26:35.

We should take note of the end of this scripture. After Peter voiced out his heart, the rest said the same. They were not going to deny Jesus and will die with Him if it came to that. I believe Jesus knowing everything and what He just told them may have thought " yeah right, let's see how far this promises survive." He just told them what will happen. Whatever He had said during the times He had been with them came to pass. What were they fighting this for? It involved love and loyalty and they had to declare that.

The Scattered and The three denial
After Jesus prayers in the Garden of Gethsemane, Judas led the religious leaders, soldiers and the mob to Jesus. He betrayed Him with a kiss. All the disciples fled. "... Then all the disciples forsook Him and fled."-Matthew 26:56. That was quite quick! What happened to the promises just a while ago?
As with the story of Jesus' arrest to crucifixion, they first led Him to Caiaphas, who was the high priest

at the time. Peter went along but stayed at a distance to the high priest's courtyard. "But Peter followed Him at a distance to the high priest's courtyard. And he went in and sat with the servants to see the end. -Matthew 26:58.

As the kangaroo and illegal court proceedings was in session with false witnesses testifying and so on, a servant girl came and said that Peter was with Jesus of Nazareth. "Now Peter sat outside in the courtyard. And a servant girl came to him, saying, "You also were with Jesus of Galilee." But he denied it before them all, saying, "I do not know what you are saying."-Matthew 26:69-70.

Another person saw Peter and said the same. "But again he denied with an oath, "I do not know the Man!"-Matthew 26:72.

A while later someone else identified him with Jesus! How good was that! "And a little later those who stood by came up and said to Peter, "Surely you also are one of them, for your speech betrays you.""-Matthew 26:73. Now Peter had heard enough!
"Then he began to curse and swear, saying, "I do not know the Man!" Immediately a rooster crowed."...!" Immediately a rooster crowed. And Peter remembered the word of Jesus who had said to him, "Before the rooster crows, you will deny Me three times." So he went out and wept bitterly.-Matthew 26:74-75.

The gospel of Luke writes that Jesus turned and looked at Peter after the rooster' crow. "And the Lord turned and looked at Peter. Then Peter remembered the word of the Lord, how He had said to him, "Before the rooster crows, you will deny Me three times.""-Luke 22:61.

We should not be quick to make promises. Let's say God willing we will be able to do so and so.

5 Trust God

Promises in Christ

God's settled promises are based in Christ. Healing is settled in heaven through Christ. Salvation is settled in heaven in Christ. Every word of God and His promises are settled in heaven in Christ. This is the reason Christ came to die to bring the new covenant in His blood. We need to recognise that we are sinners and in need of God's forgiveness. Afterwards we need to accept the gift of eternal life as we accept Jesus Christ as our personal Lord and Saviour.

To conclude this study I will give you a head start with some scriptures for you to know whatever God says you can trust Him to do. It is always good to practice searching scriptures with regards to various facets of our life. For example, we can start looking for what God says in His word concerning sickness and healing. We are fortunate to have a wide range of biblical information on the Internet to aid in research or simply searching for scriptures on specifics.

Sin and forgiveness

A child of God is also known as a saint. A saint who sin is different from a sinner who sins in the eyes of God. One is a son and the other is not. Children of God are to confess our sins to God and in return receive His forgiveness and cleansing.

"If we say that we have no sin, we deceive ourselves, and the truth is not in us. If we confess our sins, He is faithful and just to forgive us our sins and to cleanse us from all unrighteousness."-I John 1:8-9.

God cares

 Have you got any cares in your life? Are you going through situations that seem impossible to get out? Do you feel that you are in a deadly storm, which seem to be ragging forever intensifying every second? Have you been betrayed by loved ones? Is life looking as one not worth living? By following, loving Jesus and living for Him do you wonder why you have these numerous trials? Jesus has not left you. He promised never to leave nor forsake you. On top of this He want us to give Him all our cares. "casting all your care upon Him, for He cares for you."-I Peter 5:7.

Jesus promised that the Father will send the Holy Spirit in His name. He was to come and help us in all ways. This has already been fulfilled. In the book of Acts, it was recorded that He came in a spectacular way. Many from around the world who had gathered in Jerusalem for an occasion noticed his arrival. The Holy Spirit came on the day of Pentecost and still with us as our Helper. Jesus has given you His peace. You have His peace even in the midst of any trials you find yourself in.

"But the Helper, the Holy Spirit, whom the Father will send in My name, He will teach you all things, and bring to your remembrance all things that I said to you. Peace I leave with you, My peace I give to you; not as the world gives do I give to you. Let not your heart be troubled, neither let it be afraid."-John 14:26-27.

Purpose and satisfaction in life.
Do you sometimes feel down and frustrated to the extent that you feel there is no purpose or satisfaction in your life? Everything seems to be following the same routine as the society and even unbelievers seems to be doing well?

God has a plan and purpose for your life, which only you can accomplish. Social media comparisons with others will not help in any way. "For I know the thoughts that I think toward you, says the LORD, thoughts of peace and not of evil, to give you a future and a hope."-Jeremiah 29:11.

As a child of God, a Christian as we are called, we are to seek first the Kingdom of God and His righteousness. "But seek first the kingdom of God and His righteousness, and all these things shall be added to you."-Matthew 6:33.

Once that is done all the others that God know are necessities will be added to our life. This was given when Jesus taught on why we should not worry about what we will eat or drink. In the nutshell the necessities of life. Where is the next meal or money coming from? Jesus said that the Father is aware of this. ""Therefore do not worry, saying, 'What shall we eat?' or 'What shall we drink?' or 'What shall we wear?' For after all these things the Gentiles seek. For your heavenly Father knows that you need all these things."-Matthew 6:31-32

Only God can give and satisfy us with His good things because of His goodness. Nothing else can fill the vacuum He has created for this satisfaction He alone can fill.

In another teaching, the apostle Paul encourages us to be transformed in the renewal of our mind towards the things of Christ. He warns us not to be so worldly-minded as to be conformed to its system.

This is something that anyone can fall prey to without even knowing. We can be so engrossed in whatever we are involved in so much so that we may drift far from God and the things we love to do as His children without realising it. "And do not be conformed to this world, but be transformed by the renewing of your mind, that you may prove what is that good and acceptable and perfect will of God."-Romans 12:2.

Nothing is impossible to God
"For with God nothing will be impossible.""-Luke 1:37. How do we want to discuss this? We can start from the book of Genesis right through to Revelation. We cannot have enough pages and time to discuss this. We see limitations because we have limitations. The Creator of both the visible and invisible has no limitations. The Creator is above His creation and has the power to control it.

This is why we must pay attention with regards to God as His word. All His creative power and being is in His word. Taking Him at His word by faith without any shadow of a doubt opens the doors of miracles in our lives. It shatters our limitations and boundaries of impossibility. It moves us from the natural into God's realm of abundance and possibilities. We then call it a supernatural miracle.

God created everything by His word. Abraham and Sarah had a child when Sarah had passed childbearing age. In fact she was ninety years old! What about the virgin birth? The raising of the dead by Jesus and all the miracles of healing! The wind, storms and trees obey Him. In fact all His creation obey Him. With God all things are possible.

Words are powerful

"Death and life are in the power of the tongue, and those who love it will eat its fruit."-Proverbs 18:21. God does not play with words and so shall we. For example, coming to the Lord involves both the heart and our words. "..that if you confess with your mouth the Lord Jesus and believe in your heart that God has raised Him from the dead, you will be saved."-Romans 10:9

This is the principle some groups outside the church have adopted. They use words that promote 'self.' It normally sounds like you should be doing a lot to help yourself. Words that promote pride and focuses on self must be avoided. Our help comes from the Lord God Almighty. God would not have come to help us if we were able to do so. It is not a biblical doctrine.

Healing and Deliverance

"And Jesus went about all Galilee, teaching in their synagogues, preaching the gospel of the kingdom, and healing all kinds of sickness and all kinds of disease among the people."-Matthew 4:23.

As God Jesus Christ has not changed. He is the same yesterday, the same today, and will be the same tomorrow. The writer of Hebrews reminds us on this: "Jesus Christ is the same yesterday, today, and forever."-Hebrews 13:8. The same Jesus went about healing all can do the same today.

It is God's will that His children live in good health and prosper in all areas as well. "Beloved, I pray that you may prosper in all things and be in health, just as your soul prospers."-III John 1:2. This was said about a Christian called Gaius. This blessings was pronounced on him as he walked in the truth. I don't see why it will not apply to us when we also walk in the truth of God's word. It is all about trusting in the word of God and living it out.

He is able to heal and deliver us from any organised physical destruction by enemies influenced by Satan. "He sent His word and healed them, and delivered them from their destructions."-Psalms 107:20.

"who Himself bore our sins in His own body on the tree, that we, having died to sins, might live for righteousness— by whose stripes you were healed."-I Peter 2:24. Healing is a big deal for God. Jesus bore our sin in His body and died on the cross. He received numerous stripes from wicked sinners. By those stripes that destroyed His physical body we get our healing.

Power over Satan

We are first encouraged to submit to God. It is the first part of the process to be able to resist him. Once that is done through the truth of the word of God, Satan flees from us.

"Therefore submit to God. Resist the devil and he will flee from you."-James 4:7

Jesus conquered Satan through His death on the cross. In the spiritual realm Jesus disarmed principalities and power and made a public display of this victory. "Having disarmed principalities and powers, He made a public spectacle of them, triumphing over them in it."-Colossians 2:15.

What did Jesus do? On the cross Jesus finished all the work He came to accomplish. When He said it was finished, it was a shout if triumph and victory. "And Jesus cried out again with a loud voice, and yielded up His spirit."-Matthew 27:50. It was what happened immediately that was part of the triumph that took place.

The tearing of the veil covering the Holy of holies in the temple was one of the evidence of Jesus' triumph. Only the high priest was permitted to enter this place once a year to offer sacrifices to atone for the people's sins. "Then, behold, the veil of the temple was torn in two from top to bottom; and the earth quaked, and the rocks were split,"-Matthew 27:51.

This act of Jesus Christ brought the end to the old covenant. He rendered the physical temple, the law and old covenant absolutely useless and void. Remember we read earlier that Jesus instituted the New Covenant in His blood during what is now known as the last Supper. The new was established so He could take away the old on the cross. This was how He demonstrated publicly disarmament of principalities and powers.

Two important areas

First of all there were some things Paul described as handwriting of accusations and debts against us. "having wiped out the handwriting of requirements that was against us, which was contrary to us. And He has taken it out of the way, having nailed it to the cross."

Colossians 2:14. These requirements were contrary to us! It kept us in bondage! Jesus wiped this out on the cross. Jesus then took what could be described as the erased page and nailed it to the cross as evidence.

Secondly, it was after this that the second part came into existence. This was the disarmament of principalities and powers. This is the part that many Christians may not have taken time to know what happened and what was done for us. Let's analyse this step-by-step.

Principalities and powers: This describes ranks of hostile angelic beings. Never used of Good angels of God.

- "For we do not wrestle against flesh and blood, but against principalities, against powers, against the rulers of the darkness of this age, against spiritual hosts of wickedness in the heavenly places.- Ephesians 6:12

- "For I am persuaded that neither death nor life, nor angels nor principalities nor powers, nor things present nor things to come,"Romans 8:38.

- "..which He worked in Christ when He raised Him from the dead and seated Him at His right hand in the heavenly places, far above all principality and power and might and dominion, and every name that is named, not only in this age but also in that which is to come."-Ephesians 1:20-21.

What happened? The good news is that because of what Jesus did on the cross, these wicked beings don't have the same weapons to use against God's children, Christians. The bad news is that they can use it against those who are not in Christ Jesus. The same reason we should speak to all about giving their lives to Christ.

Stripping of power
Looking at what Jesus did on the cross, there were also powers behind the scenes that worked and were demonstrated physically. During Jesus' time the following powers were in existence.

- ◆ Rome: Rome was the greatest power on earth at the time.
- ◆ Government: Rome was the greatest governmental power ruling Israel at the time.
- ◆ Religious power: Judaism was the greatest religious power.
- ◆ Combination: The combination of the greatest religious and greatest political powers conspired to put the Son of God on the cross based on false testimonies and false court proceedings.

What we may not have considered is this; Jesus took the spiritual powers behind these two earthly institutions stripped them as well. How would the high priest feel when he heard the veil concealing the Holy of holies have torn from top to bottom? All the people in the temple at the time could now see whatever was there!

Jesus stripped them of their power and publicly triumphed over them! From Paul's account, it would appear that Satan and his demons may have thought they have won by crucifying the incarnate Creator of all. On the contrary, they realised that they had actually lost all their weapons and armour they can use against Jesus Christ and His followers, God's children.

This part of the divine plan took Satan and his representatives, the rulers of the earth he influenced by surprise. Remember Satan is not God's equal. He was created and due to pride and sin, now a fallen foe.

Paul wrote that if both Satan and the religious and political leaders knew putting the Son of God to death would result in their total defeat and public humiliation, they would have refrained. "But we speak the wisdom of God in a mystery, the hidden wisdom which God ordained before the ages for our glory, which none of the rulers of this age knew; for had they known, they would not have crucified the Lord of glory."-I Corinthians 2:7-8.

The Christian should not be afraid of these wicked forces. Although disarmed there are two things the demonic spirits are still able to use, their ability to create fear and to deceive. These are effective 'weapon' but not as tangible as the ones Jesus wiped out and stripped them. These evil spirits can only have power over us if we allow them by believing in the devil's lie and become fearful. Other than that we have been given the most powerful weapon, which is the use of the name of Jesus Christ. I believe that the public spectacle Jesus made after defeating the demons was more humiliating. Something we can remind them.

Walk in this victory that Christ has won for you. No weapon formed against us will prosper. Walk in the truth and Satan's lies will not overcome this powerful truth. Light will always overcome darkness. On the cross Jesus disarmed principalities and powers, triumphed over them and made a public display of their defeat.

Jesus knew the great victory He was about to accomplish for us. No wonder He said we should take heart at the face of tribulations in the world. The reason was that we have His peace and the knowledge that He has already overcome the world system. This is the defeat we just studied. "These things I have spoken to you, that in Me you may have peace. In the world you will have tribulation; but be of good cheer, I have overcome the world.""-John 16:33.

Conclusion

God is always with you. With all what we have studied together with the entire Bible, God's message to His children is still the same, I am with you. We must recognise this always. It is not a feeling, but His presence. We should acknowledge this always and see the difference that this will make in our life. It is for lack of knowledge that God's people perish. Let's stop perishing and start getting His knowledge and practice it.

"Fear not, for I am with you; be not dismayed, for I am your God. I will strengthen you, Yes, I will help you, I will uphold you with My righteous right hand.' ...For I, the LORD your God, will hold your right hand, Saying to you, 'Fear not, I will help you.'"-Isaiah 41:10, 13.

Reference
1. Hebrew for Christians. Sign of the almond tree. Meaning of almond. https://www.hebrew4christians.com/Holidays/Winter_Holidays/Tu_B_shevat/Almond_Tree/almond_tree.html. (accesses 11 jul 2020)
2. Robert J Morgan. Jeremiah's Seventy years. 28 Feb 2016. https://www.robertjmorgan.com/uncategorized/jeremiahs-seventy-years/
3. David Treybig. Life, hope & truth. Daniel 9: The seventy years prophecy of Jeremiah. https://lifehopeandtruth.com/prophecy/understanding-the-book-of-daniel/daniel-9/ (Accessed 13 July 2020)
4. Merrimack-Webster dictionary. Settled. https://www.merriam-webster.com/dictionary/settle (Accessed September 6 2020)
5. Guzik, David. Enduring a Word. Disarmed. 2015. https://enduringword.com/disarmed/

www.ingramcontent.com/pod-product-compliance
Lightning Source LLC
Chambersburg PA
CBHW061338120726
48001CB00002B/932